Meet the Dragon Slayers

Julia Campbell

Previously published as DRAGON SLAYERS TO THE RESCUE for *READ 180*.
Portions of the text have been edited to meet
System 44 program-specific phonics and vocabulary requirements.

ISBN   978-0-545-06012-7
(meets NASTA specifications)

6 7 8 9 10   113   25 24 23 22 21 20 19 18 17 16

4510002381

Contents

1 **accident** *noun*
Something that goes wrong without warning.

*They had a bad car **accident**.*

2 **crew** *noun*
A group or team.

*A **crew** of firefighters put out a fire.*

3

emergency *noun*
A sudden and dangerous situation that people have to take care of quickly.

*The workers raced to the scene of the **emergency**.*

4 **respond** *verb*
To react to something.

*The firefighters must **respond** to a fire.*

5 **training** *noun*
The studying you do to learn a skill.

*The girls need **training** to help sick people.*

6 **volunteer** *noun*
Someone who works for free.

*I am a **volunteer** at a hospital.*

Let's get this guy to the hospital!

5

CHAPTER 1

Rescue Workers

These teens are heroes.

The Dragon Slayers are a team of **volunteers**. They work in Aniak, Alaska. All of the Slayers are teens.

The teens **respond** to **emergencies**. They fight fires. They rescue people who have had **accidents**. They help people who are sick. They find people who are lost.

How did the Dragon Slayers get their name? The word "slaying" means "killing." In old stories, heroes slayed dragons. The

The crew uses this sled when there is snow. It snows a lot in Alaska.

ALASKA
Juneau

work was hard. The work was dangerous. So is the work these teens do.

Why does Aniak need the teens? The town is deep in the wild. There are rivers on all sides. No roads lead to Aniak. You need a plane or boat to get there. Sometimes, there are emergencies in Aniak. It used to take too long for help to come.

Then, fire chief Pete Brown had an idea. He would start his own fire and rescue **crew**. Brown didn't have money to pay a crew. So he got teens to volunteer.

Today, 3000 people depend on the Slayers. The team gets calls for help day and night. They respond to over 350 calls per year.

The Dragon Slayers mostly serve Aniak. Sometimes, they help other towns, too. They help out 15 other rescue teams in the area. In fact, these teams got started because of the Dragon Slayers. Beginning the Dragon Slayers was a great idea. So other towns copied it!

React

Does a rescue crew have an easy job in a place like Aniak? Why or why not?

CHAPTER 2

Becoming a Slayer

The training is tough.

How do you become a Dragon Slayer? It takes 200 hours of **training.** The training is hard work. Police and firefighters get the same training.

Volunteers learn a lot. They learn how to respond to accidents quickly. They learn how to help injured people.

When someone is hurt, the Slayers work quickly. They check out the person. They check for two main things first.

Chief Pete Brown trains Dragon Slayers. He uses a dummy. He puts a breathing tube into the dummy.

They check for breathing. They check for a heartbeat. Sometimes, the person's heart or breathing has stopped. Then the Slayers try CPR. That's a way to start someone's heart. It's also a way to help a person breathe.

The Slayers also try to stop any bleeding. They can check for broken bones, too.

Some people have been out in the cold too long. The Dragon Slayers learn how to help them.

And the Slayers don't just learn to help people. They learn to fight fires, too!

"At first the training is really hard," says one Slayer. "But you know you'll be saving lives with what you learn."

The hard training pays off. Then the Slayers start sharing what they know. They train other volunteers. They teach at a training camp in the summer. They train volunteers from all over Alaska!

React

Does the Dragon Slayers' training sound interesting? Why or why not?

CHAPTER 3

Emergency!

Can the Slayers save a life?

It was a cold night in December. Three boys were zipping down the road on snowmobiles. Snow was falling fast. It was so thick the boys could barely see.

The boys charged into a cloud of snow. A truck was hidden in the snow. The boys didn't see it. It was too late to stop. One boy crashed into the truck.

The boy was badly hurt. His head was bleeding. It was a big emergency.

The crew responds quickly to each call.

Quickly, the other boys called for help. They called the Dragon Slayers. Four teens responded. Gary, Alec, Candi, and Garrett went running to the scene.

The Slayers knew the accident was bad. But the sight of the injured boy was shocking. He had broken his jaw, skull, and neck. The breaks were bad.

The Slayers weren't sure he would make it. Still, they didn't panic. They knew what to do. They made sure the boy was breathing. They stopped his bleeding.

The boy needed to get to a hospital. The only way there was by plane. But the snow was too heavy. A plane couldn't come.

The Slayers stayed up all night with the boy. He was in great pain. The teens were kind to him. They did everything they could to help him.

After 12 hours, a plane came. It took the boy to the hospital. Would he survive? At last, news came from the hospital. The boy would live! The Slayers were thrilled. Their training had paid off.

"Those kids did a lot of good work that night!" Chief Brown says.

Life Lessons

Dragon Slayers never forget.

The Slayers' stories don't end after high school. Many get jobs saving lives.

Slayer Mariah Brown is Chief Brown's daughter. Today, she is a navy medic. Being a Slayer prepared her for her job.

Shigone Beghail was a Slayer. Now she's a medic in Iraq. That's a long way from Alaska. Yet, her Dragon Slayer training helps her every day. They were lessons for a lifetime.

Think. Talk. Write.

Would you want to be a Dragon Slayer? Why or why not?

Use this sentence starter to talk or write about your answer.

> I would/would not want to be a Dragon Slayer because ...

Re-read.

Look for answers to these questions.

> Why did Pete Brown start the Dragon Slayers?
>
> How are some Dragon Slayers using their training in their adult jobs?